poetry

rhian
edwards

tall-lighthouse

for Hugo

Acknowledgements and thanks are due
to the editors of Poetry Wales, Pen Pusher,
the Delinquent and Stand where some of these
poems, or versions of them, were first published.

cover image: mat redvers

cover photo: peter simkin

© Rhian Edwards 2008
Rhian Edwards has asserted her right under
the Copyright, Design and Patents Act 1988
to be identified as the author of this work.

ISBN 978 1 904551 47 8

published by
tall-lighthouse
www.tall-lighthouse.co.uk

contents

Suitcase	1
Sick bed	2
Petra	3
Crossed	4
Sheer	5
Sea of her	6
Gravy	6
Back to bed	7
The ruins	8
Fib	8
Eyeful	8
Unmentionable	9
The Welshman who couldn't sing	10
Quotidian	12
Hitched	13
Marital visit	14

Suitcase

A ventriloquist's doll –
dangling limbs, a fixed
laughing grin, unable to talk

back, unable to blink without
the perch of your knee.
You fold me in at the waist

my feet kicking my ears,
squeezed in a suitcase
and shelved out of sight

till I wake to the rattling,
the sound of your wife hanging
her blouses beneath me.

Sick bed

It went as far as the eyes,
stirred something up, stitching them shut.

The morning I woke to the immediate black,
eyelids padlocked, I howled for myself.

The tears had nowhere to go, they stayed put,
dammed up against thin walls of skin.

In the blacked-out room, you let
me lie on you again.

You dabbed and circled pink ointment
into the mohair itch of my body,

while I wriggled, sickened
most at being put back in nappies.

You touched my cheek and palms
with the cool plastic of toys.

I heard you in the doorway, watching
with your hand on your hip.

You did the crying for me,
smoking cigarettes in prayer.

Petra

Remember when Tommo found the library
and fingered out that Blue Peter classic
Petra: A Dog For All Seasons?
That title clung to you like a Kick Me sign
sticky-taped to the back of your blazer.

You took your pseudonym well –
stormed the school like Boudicca –
all matronly bounce and mucky blonde hair,
a dirty fat smile for the corridors,
purple Doc Martens tippexed with stars.

Both your parents were vicars,
built like polar bears and born in their cardigans.
They let you say *fucking* before everything,
blessed you with the biggest room in the vicarage,
you even got your own kettle and teabags
which made you practically an adult.

But how did you sleep in that room Petra
Hawksworth amongst spread-eagled sheet music,
the straggle of elephantine bras and unwanted
pants that puddled the floor?
It was a wonder you could revise
in the thick of your circus of baby-oiled men
chewing-gum-tacked to the walls.

Remember the night of the harvest festival
when your soprano solo made the music
                                      teacher weep?
At David Newman's party at his father's hotel,
you came into your own, realised
the Petra you hankered for.

That was the night your boobs came out to play.
You got off with the room, snog-hacked
a thoroughfare from kitchen to lounge,
you fell to your knees in the garden
and in the cold grass earned your fellatio wings.

Crossed

She wears her head
on the bone of his shoulder,
wraps his cold hand
in the skin of her own.

He doesn't unfold
or relent an affection,
just parks a white gaze
in the humdrum of windows.

She noses his neck,
pretends pretty sleep,
he keeps his limbs crossed,
his eyelids unbatted.

He ghosts the girl,
forgetting to want her,
as she knits a clement world
around his unwanting.

Sheer

Black hairs spear through the pale
pink wheel of my nipples,
whisker-thick to the pinch,
sprouting sheer as a thorn.

A crack in the egg,
a lash in the eye,
a smattering of black grass
marring the blanch of the moon.

Perhaps it is the fray
from the seams of my skin,
a rag doll unstitching
her two needless patches.

Eight threads puncture the thin
limpid membrane of halo,
this breast is gravid
with a hatching of spiders.

Sea of her

Head pillowed on belly
of vanilla-soaked flesh,
this skull rowed her gently
to her lappings of breath.

There, I dozed and I dreamed,
I lazed and I lounged,
in her pool of milk skin
this man practically drowned.

Gravy

We rock like a crib in a book
crowded room to pictures of your wife
grinning through the ages.

You call me *darling* and I stifle
a giggle. It's all a bit cloying
and anxious, you and me.

You start to sweat. It smells
of gravy. Wanting to be
myself, I tell you.

Back to bed

You rip off the blankets
to stop me losing the day.
I dream in epics, you see,
you think I won't wake
and might adventure without you.

I'm a drawer fully open
now something has to be touched.
You drop a kiss to the belly,
list my bits that you prize.
What a waste of good fawning
when the flattered is sleep-swooned!

The chill of your spit
and the wind you've let in
shudder me back to the room
and this ordinary morning –
all thumping in sunshine
I wish I could bin.

I abandon your bed for the bathroom
and the griffin-clawed tub,
which squats under the window,
cupping the punctured clouds of your lather.

I pussy-foot into the tepid,
the yellowed porcelain squeaks as I slide,
wheeling the hot tap with my toe
I veil my face in damp flannels
and in the snug of the soap-swamp
perfect my vanishing act.

The ruins

Sprawled in the ruins
of unperishing summer
I drowse in the lead-weighted air
and smothering pillow of sun.

Fib

Tattooed in freckles
and a smattering of features

a dangle of auburn
and a cocksure chin

I parade the fib
that will one day become me.

Eyeful

Looking me dizzy
licking me drunk
in the face of our nudity
I am not nearly naked enough.

Unmentionable

He rusts my blood,
cadavers my skin,
sweating a smile,
a jaundice-licked grin.

Hid, curled and trembling,
eyes sealed to blind,
a mock of salivas
scratch teeth down my spine.

A nocturne of moths,
bat wings in my belly,
my heart, red and fisted,
thumps in its cage to betray me.

Please hush-now this heart
to dumben my breath,
please muffle the whimpers,
the drippings of sweat.

Claw back the tears
and gnaw off this tongue,
unquiver the jaw
caesura this lung.

Die me a death
to deprive me of sense,
maim me or sleep me,
let the horror be silence.

The Welshman who couldn't sing

I'm sketching his sound,
a motorbike's rumble
or the cartoon voice
of an elderly sheepdog.
The Welshman who couldn't sing,
who could massacre a funeral hymn
with a throatful of catarrh
and a hiccup-spit of words,
a never-ending baffle
to the women of his making.

I'm scratching off a smile
on a weather-battered face,
his Brillo padded cheeks
scoured skin off my pecking lips
and a yellow-toothed snigger
that could thaw me to tears.

I'm mimicking his canon now:
food was his bible,
with lamb chop in his clutches
he purred with every gnaw,
his podgy pygmy fingers
dripping thick in minted gravy,
would wriggle in the supper air
as if knitting a potent sentence.

I'm fattening up his bones
to a torso like a turnip,
a hill of hairless belly
I climbed and conquered as a baby
and a spooned-out pit of navel
that could house an old ten-penny.

I'm giving back his limbs
two arms wooden to the hip,
sleeves of freckles to the knuckle,
fingers curled in threatless fists.
His Gypsy-dog thin legs
marched with the scurries
of an unleashed toddler,
forever, it seems, betraying
the weight he was made to haul.

Quotidian

It's all about the habits -
borrowing five more minutes
from a clock that rolls its eye
and buries its head in the pillow.

It's all about those minutes -
lips stepping the stones of your spine,
the banshee of an alarm
that brings us back to our senses.

It's all about disarray -
coffee pot wobbling on the gas hob,
toothpaste bearding my chin,
black liquid spitting at the kitchen tiling.

It's all about the hush -
laying the mug beside you,
you mumbling the dearest of thank-yous
for a drink you're unlikely to touch.

Hitched

Violent tiredness has stripped
our mouths down to this skeletal
talk and grimacing silence.

Tongues, once swaggered
with muscles of mirth, now flap
at the table, starved of all rapture.

In a bootless attempt to replenish lost
joys, you pluck from the napkin
a tale for the telling.

With a flurry of arm wags and plasticine
face, you spill all the beans
for a flicker of awe.

I dispatch a dim smile and spy
on the gossips, as the swelling dead air
rots the menu between us.

Marital visit

It's her visiting time
which presses the pause,
makes you follow me downstairs
and shepherd me out of the door.

I sigh the train South,
unearth my unwanted habits,
remind all my rooms
to smell of me again.

Like the man who threw a party
but didn't dare touch a drop,
you busy yourself in the tidying,
the rounding up of my scraps.

The ritual begins with the clearing
away of my face – foundation, lipstick,
powder, concealer, the wooden brush
cobwebbed with my unyielding knots.

Everything strewn like toys on the surface
of her kidney-shaped dressing table
is gathered and bagged as on the day
they had the nerve to arrive.

You empty the shelves of my skin –
the eczema ointments, the bottled fake tan,
the perfume you bought on a whim
that patched me in rashes.

Flicked over the edge,
my pieces topple into the dark
where they chink together
as if to toast their reunion.

Your wife lets herself in,
carries herself across the threshold,
smiles at her hallway,
sniffing me everywhere.